Written and Illustrated by Janet Jerger

Dance Teacher press

Dance Teacher Press
Seward, Nebraska

Library of Congress Control Number: 2009928000
ISBN10: 0-9816586-3-6
ISBN13: 978-0-9816586-3-6

Dance Teacher press

For more information, visit www.DanceTeacherPress.com

Printed in the United States of America

10 9 8 7 6 5 4 3 2 1

Contents

Arabesques

Body Facings

Introduction to Ballet Terminology

The ballet terms defined in this book are French. The French terms are used in ballet classes all over the world. There are slight variations from school to school, but there will be many similarities. The terms in this book will give you a good basis for understanding ballet and its terminology.

The French term is shown first.

(The pronunciation is given in parentheses.)

The translation of the French word is given in purple print.

When there is an accent that slopes up (é), the e sounds like long a.
When there is an accent that slopes down (è), the e has the short e sound.

These terms tell the direction of the leg or arm.

Devant
(duh-VAHN) = **in front**

Derrière
(deh-RYYHR) = **in back**

À la Seconde
(ah la suh-GAWND) = **to the second = to the side**

Have fun learning about ballet!

Ballet Etiquette

1. Be prompt.

You will show your desire to learn by being on time for class and ready to dance.

2. Follow the school dress code.

Tights and leotards help your teacher see your body for corrections and, when in front of the mirror, will help you to see yourself too.

3. Secure your hair neatly, up and away from the face and neck.

You do not want to be distracted by your hair while dancing.

4. Please, no chewing gum.

You are a performer, and a pleasing expression on your face is an important part of your performance.

5. Let your body language show your desire to learn.

Never lean on walls, barres, or sit down without being instructed to do so.

6. Give your complete attention to the teacher.

Do not visit during class. Dance class is a time to develop the concentration needed to be a good dancer.

7. Finish every combination.

Even if you make a mistake, keep trying. Continue working until the music stops or you have gone all the way across the floor.

8. Accept corrections with grace and a smile.

Try to mark through the correction with the teacher as it is given.

9. Always practice as if you are performing for an audience.

Adopting this attitude will push you to be your best.

10. Thank the teacher at the end of class.

You may show your appreciation with a curtsy, clapping, or simply saying "thank you."

Good manners create a good learning environment and help you develop the discipline to be a wonderful dancer.

Hands and Turnout

Beautiful hands are an important part of ballet.
In most positions the hands are curved and continue in the curved line of the arm. The middle finger curves in toward the thumb and the other three fingers are slightly less curved. The fingers are just slightly apart from each other.
When hands are in arabesque, the line of the arm and hands is straighter. The palms are down and the fingers are extended forward in the line of the arm. The middle finger is still the closest to the thumb, while the other fingers reach forward.

A note about turn-out.
You may have noticed that the toes are "turned out" in the five positions. A perfect first position could look like this:
But it would be incorrect to turn-out the toes this much unless the whole leg is turned out from the hip. This takes time and practice. While you are learning, your first position might look like this:
In a demi or grand plié, always make sure your knees open over your toes. This is a good way to check where your toes should go. Only open your toes as much as you can open your knees.

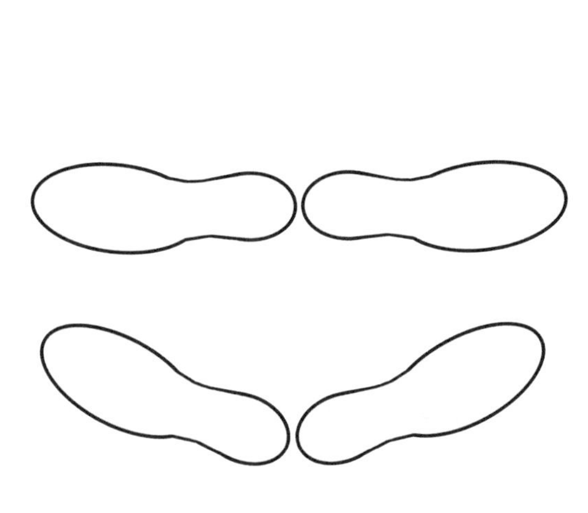

Ballet Barre

This section of the book shows you the five positions of ballet and the basic movements practiced at the ballet barre. Ballet barre work is usually at the beginning of a ballet class. These exercises give you the foundation for all ballet steps. Holding on to a ballet barre helps you to balance as you work on each movement. After the teacher explains the exercise, stand tall in the given position and wait quietly for the music to begin. When it is time to change sides, always turn toward the barre.

Additional sections in a ballet class.

Adagio - *(ad-DAHZH-ee-oh)* - **Slowly.**

In an Adagio the dancer practices slow and controlled movements. Adagio is practiced in the center of the room. Adagio may consist of port de bras (arm movements) and other slow movements to practice strength and balance.

Petite Allegro - *(puh-TEET ah-lay-GROH)* - **Small brisk and lively.**

A wide variety of small jumps, transitional movements and pirouettes are practiced in the center.

Grand Allegro - *(grahnd ah-lay-GROH)* - **Large brisk and lively.**

Grand Allegro is often practiced "from the corner" where the dancers will go in small groups from the back corner diagonally across the room. Grand allegro may include large jumps, transitional steps, waltzes and turns.

Your teacher may add stretching, or other additional sections to your class.

The Five Positions

In ballet there are five positions of the feet. In French they say, "positions des pieds."
(paw-zee-SYAWN day pyay)

There are also five positions of the arms. In French they say, "positions des bras."
(paw-zee-SYAWN day brah)

Première Position

(pruh-MYEHR paw-zee-SYAWN)

First Position

The heels are together. The legs are turned out. First position arms are also called "en avant" meaning forward.

Seconde Position

(suh-GAWND paw-zee-SYAWN)

Second Position

The feet are on the same line spaced by a length one and a half times the student's foot.

Troisième Position
(trwah-ZYEM paw-zee-SYAWN)

Third Position

One foot is in front of the other, the front heel touches the middle of the back foot.

Quatrième Position
(ka-tree-EM paw-zee-SYAWN)

Fourth Position

The feet are parallel, one foot in front of the other and one foot length apart.

Cinquième Position
(sen-KYEM paw-zee-SYAWN)

Fifth Position

The feet are crossed so that the heel of the front foot touches the toe on the back foot. Fifth position arms are also called "en haut" meaning high.

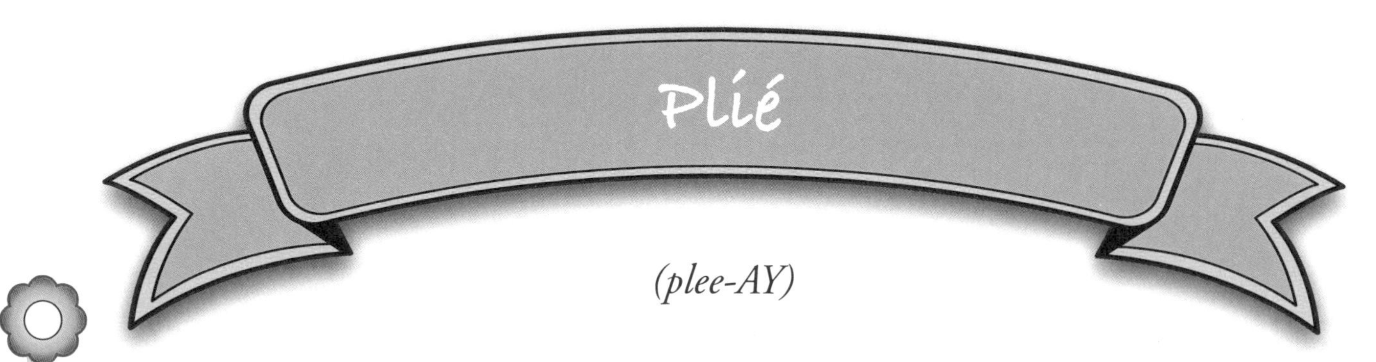

Plié

(plee-AY)

Demi-plié

(duh-MEE- plee-AY)

Small bending.

Half bending of the knees. Gently bend the knees opening to the sides with knees over the toes. The heels always stay on the ground in demi-plié.

Grand Plié

(grahn plee-AY)

Large bending.

Bend the knees slowly out to the sides as the body lowers. The heels stay on the floor as long as possible and then lift as the body continues to go lower. Press the heels to the floor as the body comes back up. The heels always stay on the floor in second position grand plié.

Pliés may be done in any of the 5 positions of the feet.

Battement Tendu

(bat-MAHN tahn DEW)

Battement stretched.

The working foot slides out from first or fifth position to a fully pointed foot to the front, side, or back. It then returns to original position. The toe never leaves the floor. Battement Tendu is done to make the feet and ankles strong and flexible.

Battement is a word used in association with many ballet words. In a battement the working leg usually moves away from and then back to the standing leg.

Battement Dégagé

(bat-MAHN day-ga-ZHAY)

Battement disengaged.

Similar to tendu but quicker. The working foot passes through tendu and rises from the floor about 4 inches. The leg moves quickly with a strong accent. Dégagé prepares the dancer for the strength and quickness required in jumping.

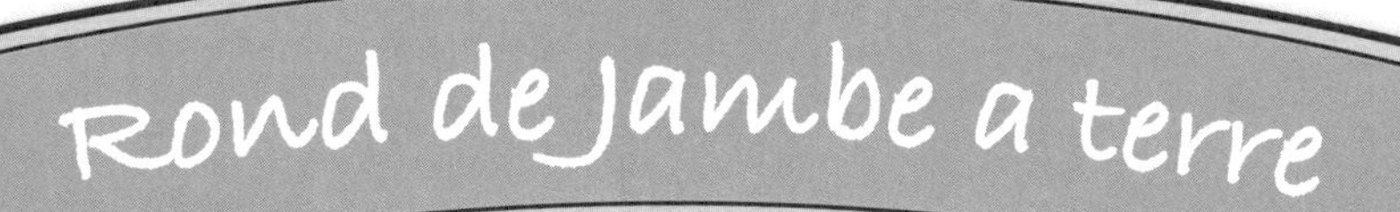

(rawn duh zhahnb ah tehr)

Round of the leg on the ground.
The leg extends to the front, slides in a circular motion to the side, around to the back, and comes to first position. The toe never leaves the floor. (This direction is en dehors (outside).) Rond de jambe may also be done from the back around to the side and to the front. (This direction is en dedans (inside).) Rond de jambe works on the rotation of the hip for increased range of motion.

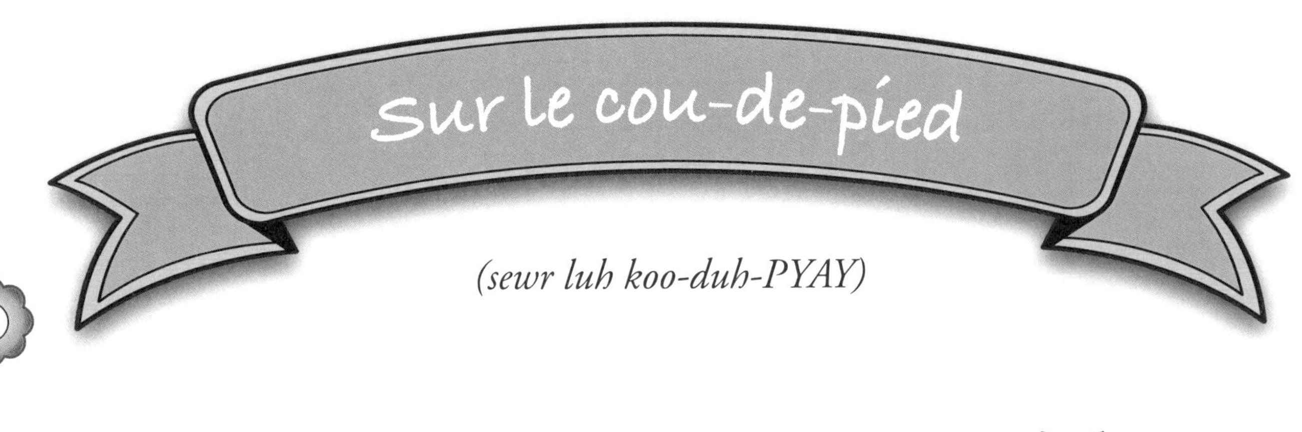

(sewr luh koo-duh-PYAY)

cou-de-pied devant fully stretched

cou-de-pied derrière fully stretched

sur le cou-de-pied wrapped

On the neck of the foot.

Sur le cou-de-pied is a position in which the working leg touches the neck of the foot of the standing leg. The neck of the foot is between the ankle and the base of the calf, or two inches above the ankle. The foot may be pointed as pictured in the illustrations, or flexed as in the next exercise frappé.

Many teachers say coupé for this position.

Battement Frappé

(bat-MAHN fra-PAY)

Battement struck.

1. The foot begins in a flexed position at the ankle (sur le cou-de-pied).
2. The ball of the foot strikes the floor as the leg extends to dégagé height.
3. The foot does not strike the floor as it returns to the ankle.

Passé

(pah-SAY)

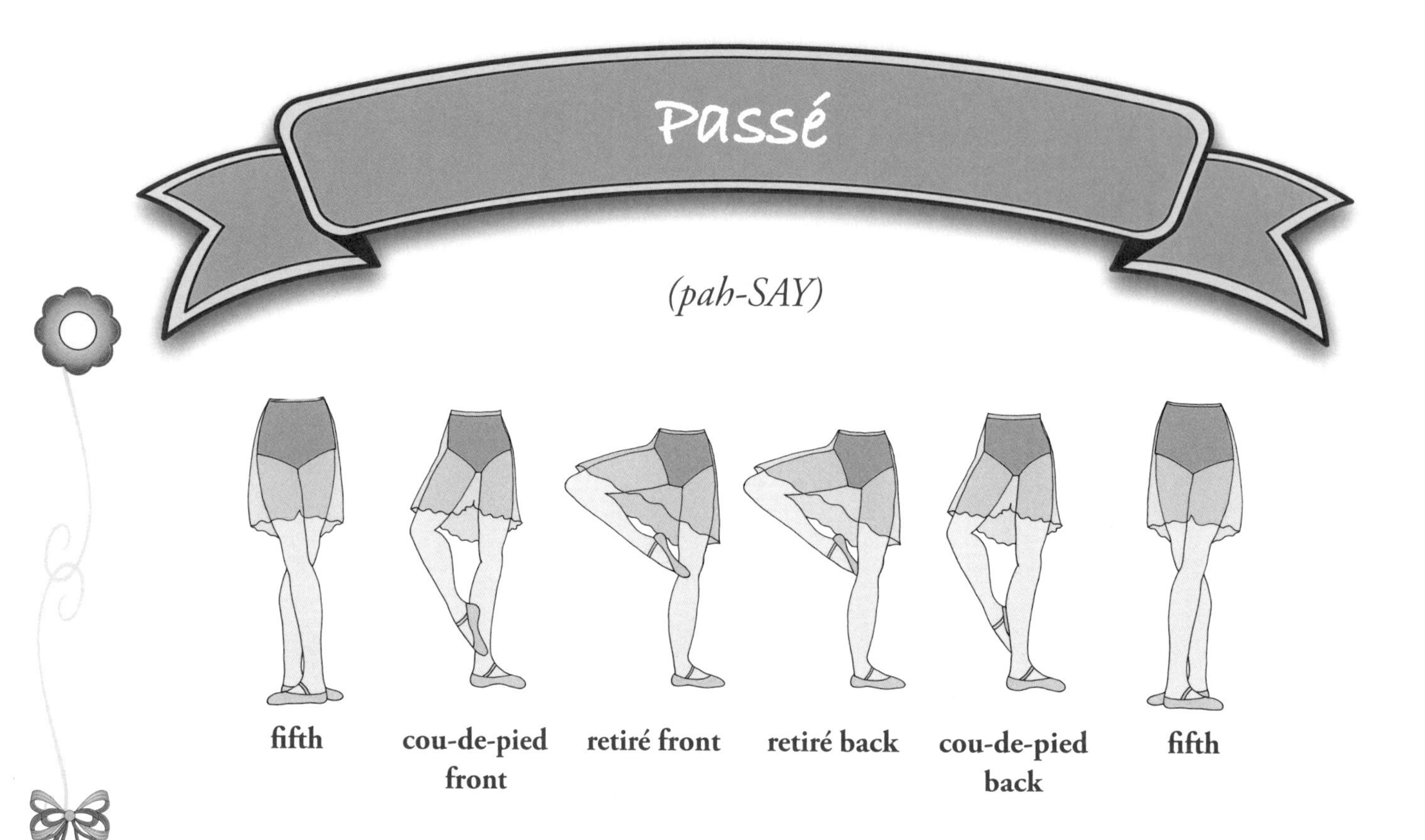

Passed.

In passé the foot of the working leg passes by the knee of the standing leg.

1. Illustrated is the exercise passé changée where the leg goes through the above positions to change the fifth position.
2. Passé is used to describe any movement where the toe of one leg passes by the knee of the other leg while moving from one position to the other. (See passé développé on page 16.)
3. Some teachers may call the position retiré front "passé."

Fondu

(fawn-DEW)

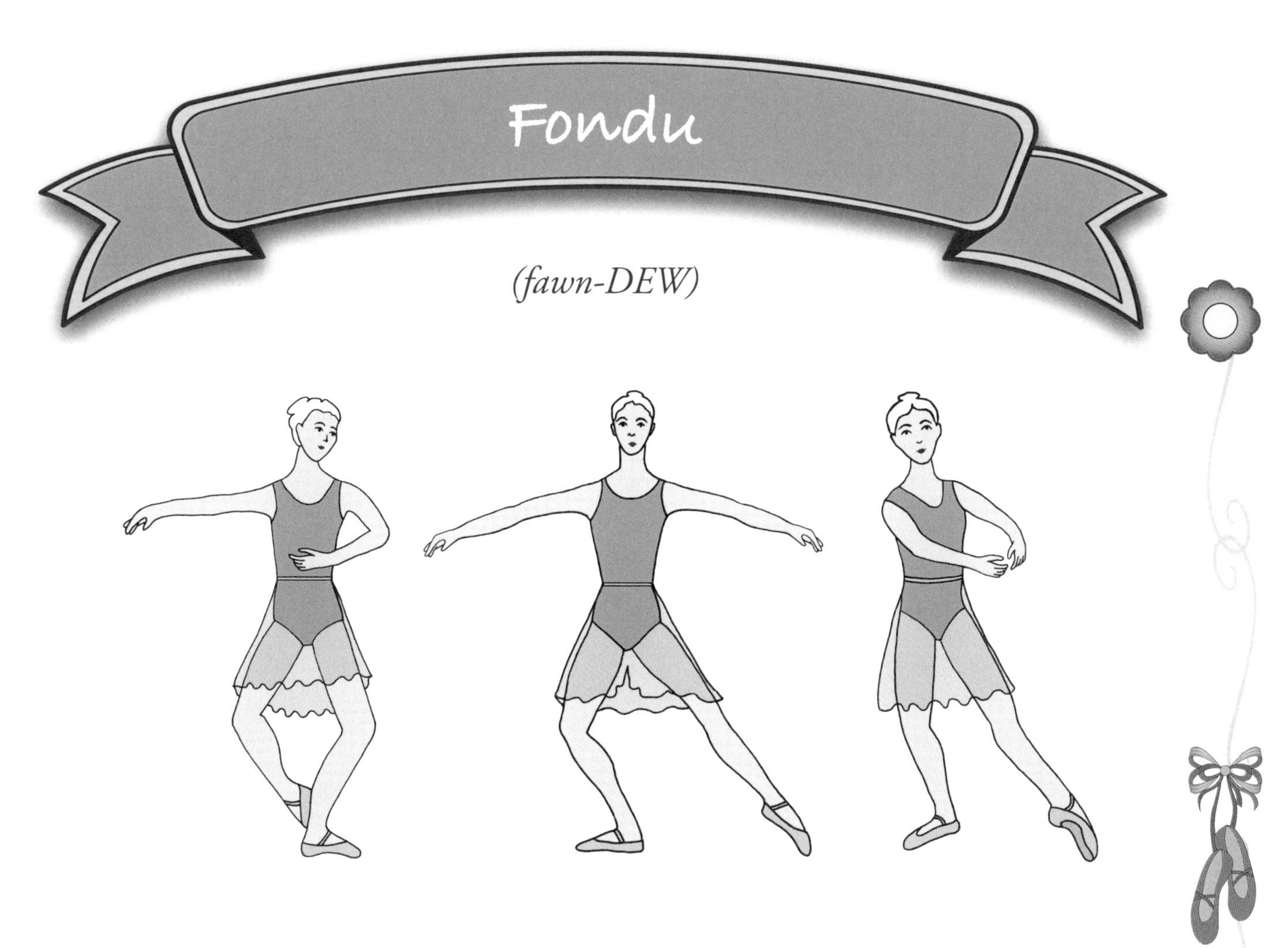

Sinking down.

Fondu simply means to plié on one leg. The other leg may be placed in any position while in fondu. Above are three different examples of fondu. Fondu is done to practice the balance needed when taking off and landing from jumps.

Passé Développé

(pah-SAY dayv-law-PAY)

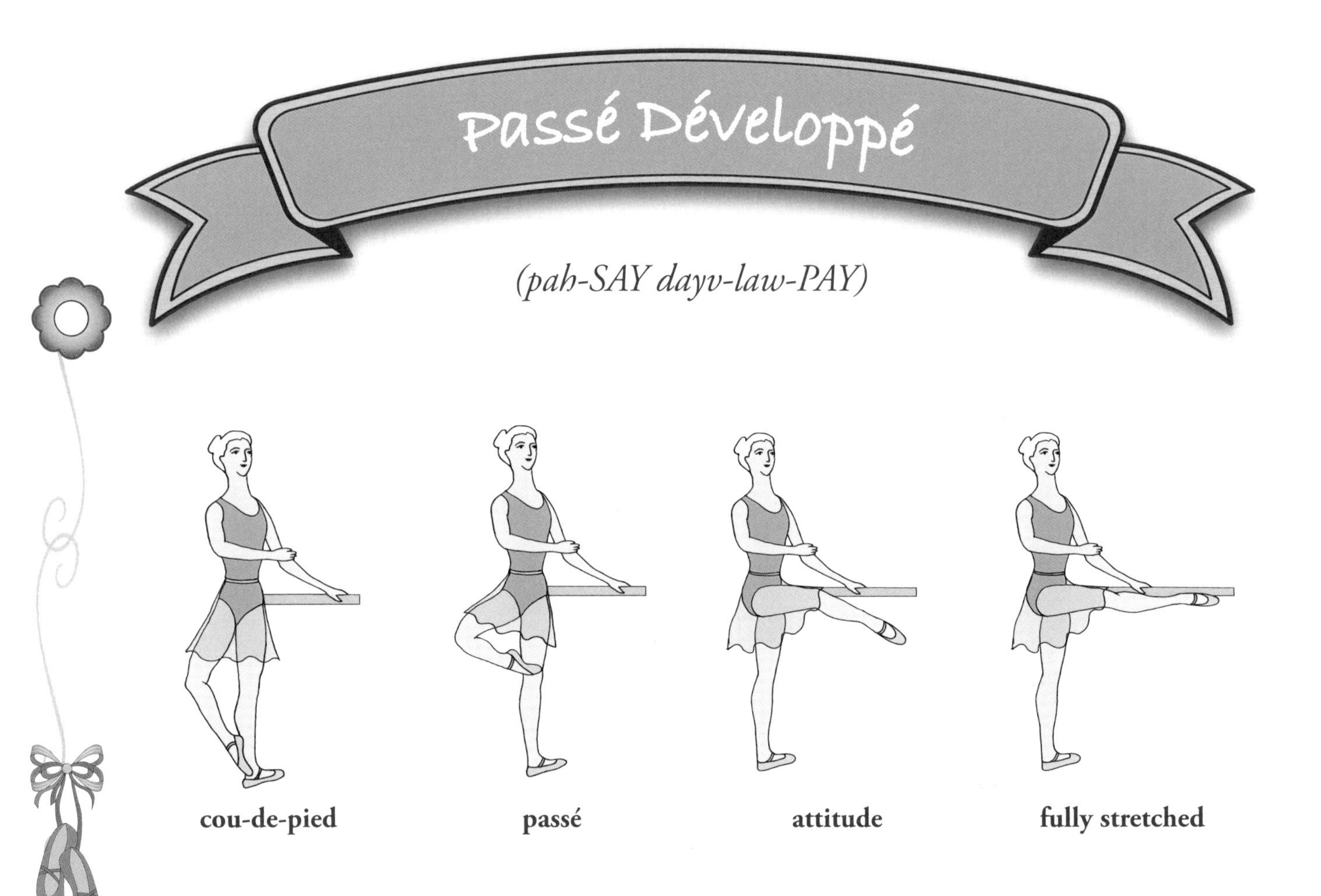

Passed developed.

Passé développé is a slow and controlled movement. The knee points sideways and the working foot draws slowly up the standing leg and extends to the front, side, or back. The leg will go through cou-de-pied, passé, and attitude before extending. Attitude is a slightly bent position between passé and fully extended.

Rond de Jambe en l'air

(rawn duh zhahnb ahn lehr)

en dehors - draw your toe straight in toward the knee, then a little forward and out.

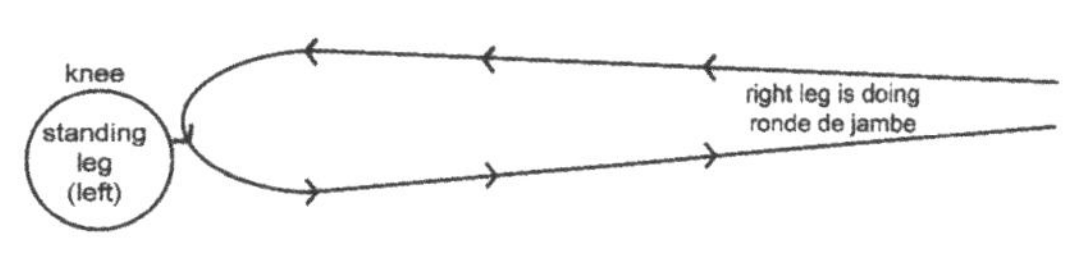

en dedans - draw your toe slightly in front of the knee, then to the knee and out.

Round of the leg in the air.

Rond de jambe en l'air is like drawing a rain drop in the air with your toe. The leg begins extended à la seconde. Leaving the thigh in place, bring the toe inward toward the standing leg in a circular motion, and extend back to à la seconde. Rond de jambe can be done at various heights.

(grahn rawn duh zhahnb)

Large round of the leg.
Illustrated at 90º (hip height).

1. En dehors. **Outside.** The leg is extended at 90º devant. Smoothly carry the leg to à la seconde, and then on to derrière. Maintain a consistent height and turnout.
2. En dedans. **Inside.** Begin with the leg is extended derrière. Smoothly carry the leg to à la seconde and then to devant.

Grand Battement

(grahn bat-MAHN)

Large Beating.

The working leg is raised quickly to its highest height to the front, back, or side. And then it returns to a closed position just as quickly. The leg should pass through the tendu ascending and descending. Both legs stay straight in a grand battement. This movement is done to prepare for large jumps and leaps.

Relevé and Sous-sus

Relevé
(ruhl-VAY)

Raised. Relevé is to rise up on to demi-pointes (balls of the feet) in slippers or on to full pointes in toe shoes. You may relevé in any position on one or two feet.

Sous-sus
(soo-SEW)

Under-over. Sous-sus is a special relevé in fifth position. Spring up on to the demi-pointes or pointes drawing the legs together and the toes under so the feet fit closely together.

Center Movements

In this section are jumps and transitional steps that move.
These terms tell the direction the body will move.

en Avant - *(ah na-VAHN)* - **Forward.**

en Arrière - *(ah na-RYYHR)* - **Backward.**

de Coté - *(duh koh-TAY)* - **Sideways.**

Sauté - *(soh-TAY)* - **Jumped or jumping.**
Sauté is a jump from two feet to two feet.

Temps levé - *(tahn luh-VAY)* - **Time raised.**
Temps levé is a hop on one foot which may be done in any position.

Battu - *(ba-TEW)* - **Beaten.**
Many jumps can be embellished with a battu (or beat).
The legs cross and beat together while in the air.

Sautés always begin and end in plié.

Changement de Pieds

(shahnzh-MAHN duh pyay)

Change of feet.

Jump from fifth position plié and extend the legs and the toes in the air. To finish land in fifth position plié with the other foot in front.

Escaping movement jumping.
Échappé sauté is two jumps in a row. Begin in fifth demi-plié, jump up and land in seconde position plié. Next jump up and land in fifth plié with the other foot in front.

Entrechat Trois

(ahn-truh-SHAH trwah)

Braided three times.

Jump up from fifth position plié, squeeze (beat) the thighs together in sous-sus in the air. Change the legs, and land on one foot with the other in cou-de-pied.

(ahn-truh-SHAH Ka-truh)

Braided four times.

Jump from fifth plié, change the legs two times in the air and land in your original fifth. The legs are fully extended as they cross or beat in the air.

Odd numbered entrechats land on one foot, even numbered entrechats land on two feet.

Jeté

(zhuh-TAY)

Thrown.

Jeté is a jump from one foot to one foot. The working leg brushes along the floor and out to dégagé height as the standing leg springs up into the air. This illustration shows jeté over where the back leg comes over and lands front, with the other leg in cou-de-pied back. In jeté under the front leg will brush side and land back with the other leg in cou-de-pied front.

Assemblé

(ah-sahm-BLAY)

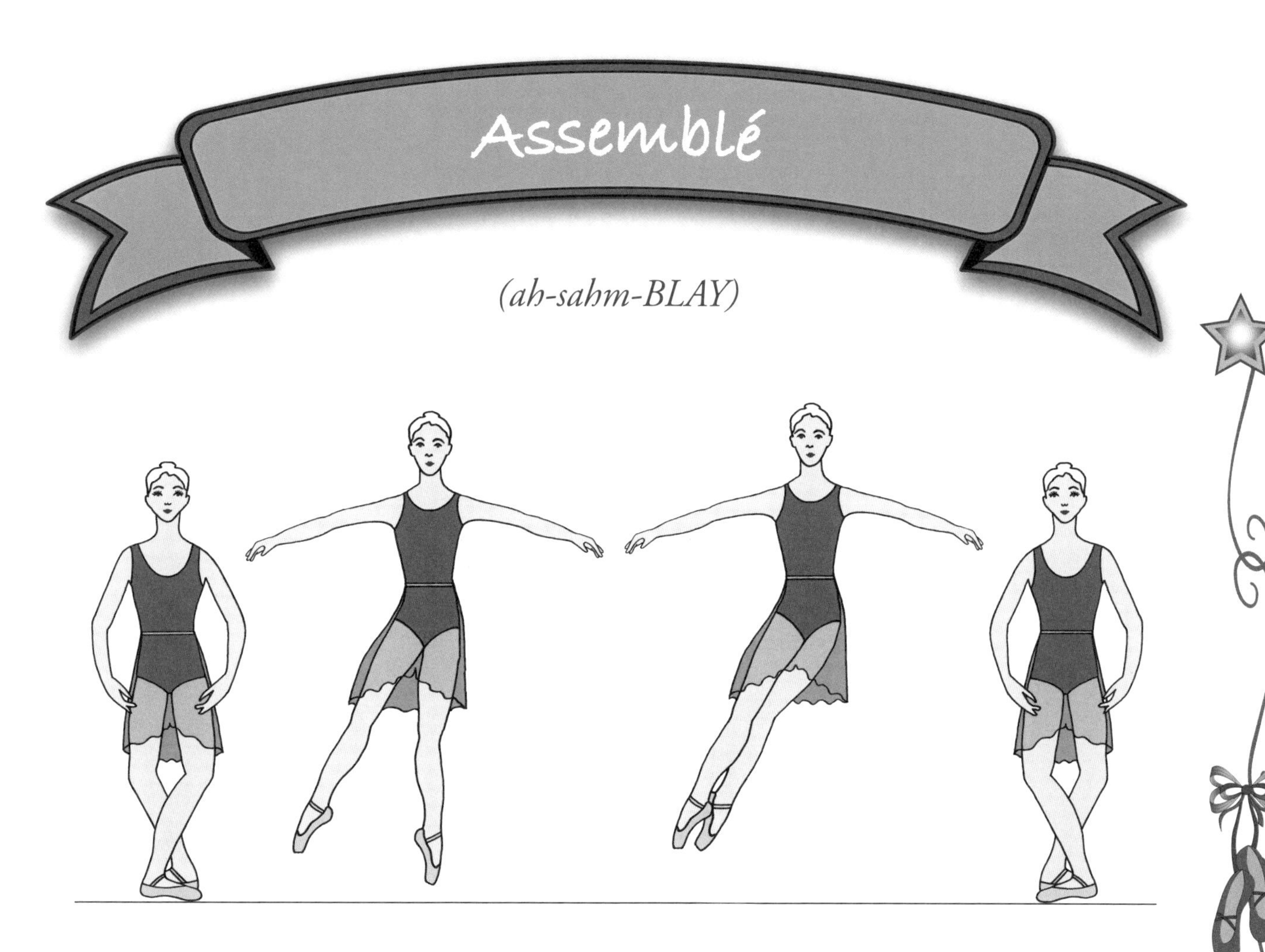

Assembled.

Assemblé is a jump from one foot to two feet. The working leg brushes along the floor and out to dégagé height as the standing leg springs into the air and meets the working leg. The legs land together in fifth position plié. Assemblé can go many directions—front, back, over, under and more. This illustration shows assemblé over: the back leg brushes side, comes over and lands front. In assemblé under the front leg will brush side and land back.

Chassé

(sha-SAY)

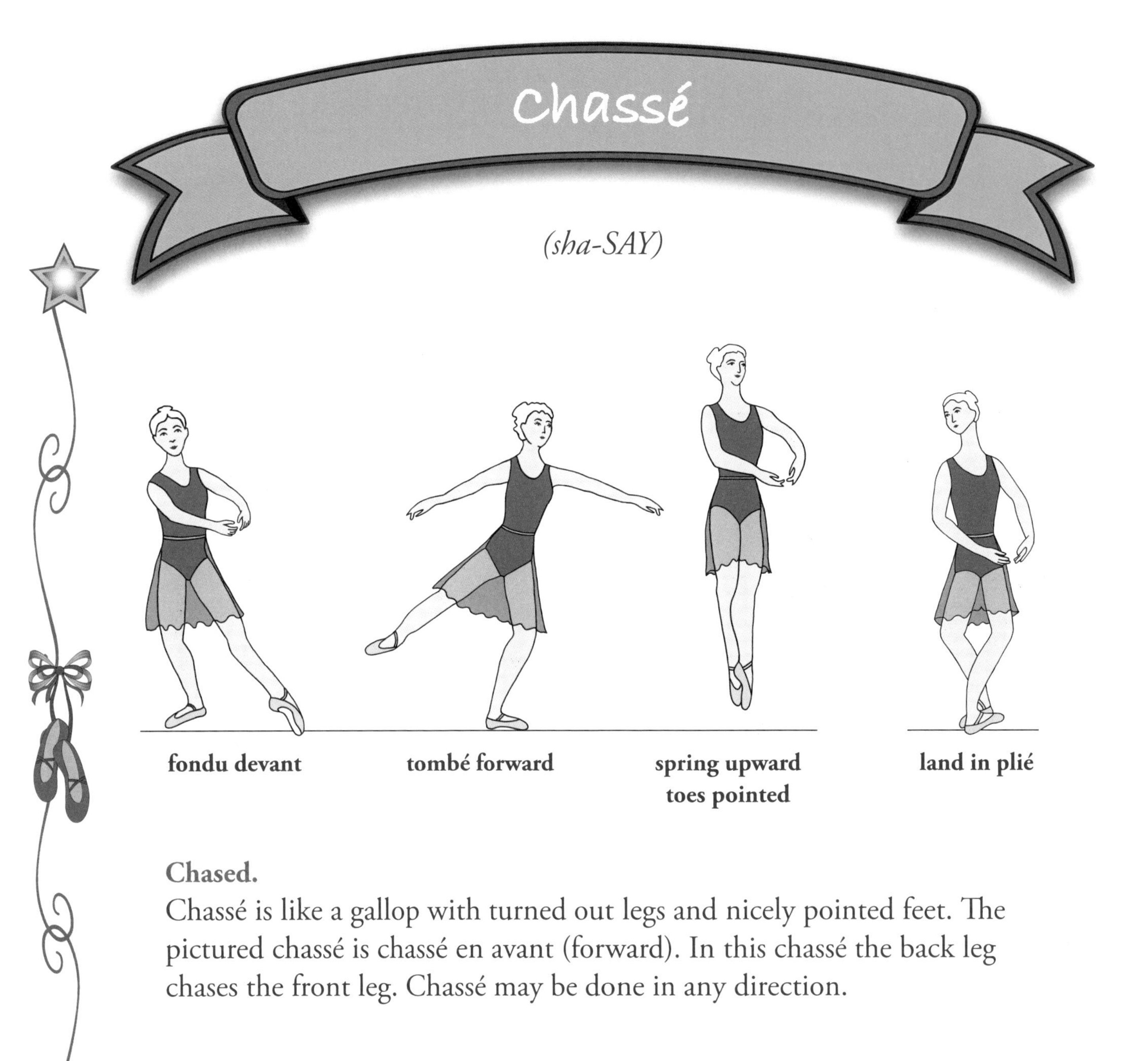

Chased.

Chassé is like a gallop with turned out legs and nicely pointed feet. The pictured chassé is chassé en avant (forward). In this chassé the back leg chases the front leg. Chassé may be done in any direction.

Glissade

(glee-SAHD)

Glide.

Glissade is a traveling or linking step from fifth position to fifth position. It may be executed in any direction. Pictured is glissade de côté under. Begin with a demi plié in fifth, slide the front foot out to the side and jump into the air stretching both legs, the first foot reaches the floor and lands in fondu, and the second leg closes fifth front plié.

Pas de Chat

(pah duh shah)

Step of the Cat.

Begin in fifth with the right foot derrière. Spring up and bring the right leg to retiré, immediately bring the left leg up to match. Hold this pose briefly in the air. Land with the right leg first and immediately close the left foot in front in fifth.

As with all jumps—begin and end in demi-plié.

Pas de Bourrée

(pah duh boo-RAY)

1 - back

2 - side

3 - front

Bourrée step.

Pas de bourrée is a linking step that can go in many directions.

Dessous (under): step back, side, front (pictured above)

Dessus (over): step front, side, back

Devant (front): step front, side, front

Derriere (back): step back, side, back

En tournant (in turning)

On count 3 you may also lower to fifth plié, or to fondu with cou-de-pied.

Bourrée

(boo-RAY)

Bourrée

Bourrée is a traveling step where the female dancer seems to be gliding along the floor. It can be done on demi-pointe (half toe) or on pointe. You can bourrée in any direction. Illustrated is bourrée de côté. Begin in sous-sus and reach across even further with your back leg, now move your front foot so you are in fifth position again. Continue with many of these quick little steps always keeping the legs crossed.

Large Jumps and Pirouettes

In this section we have some more advanced movements. The large jumps are often used in the grand allegro section of class. Pirouettes and turns may be used in adagio, petite allegro or grand allegro combinations.

Sissonne

(see-SAWN)

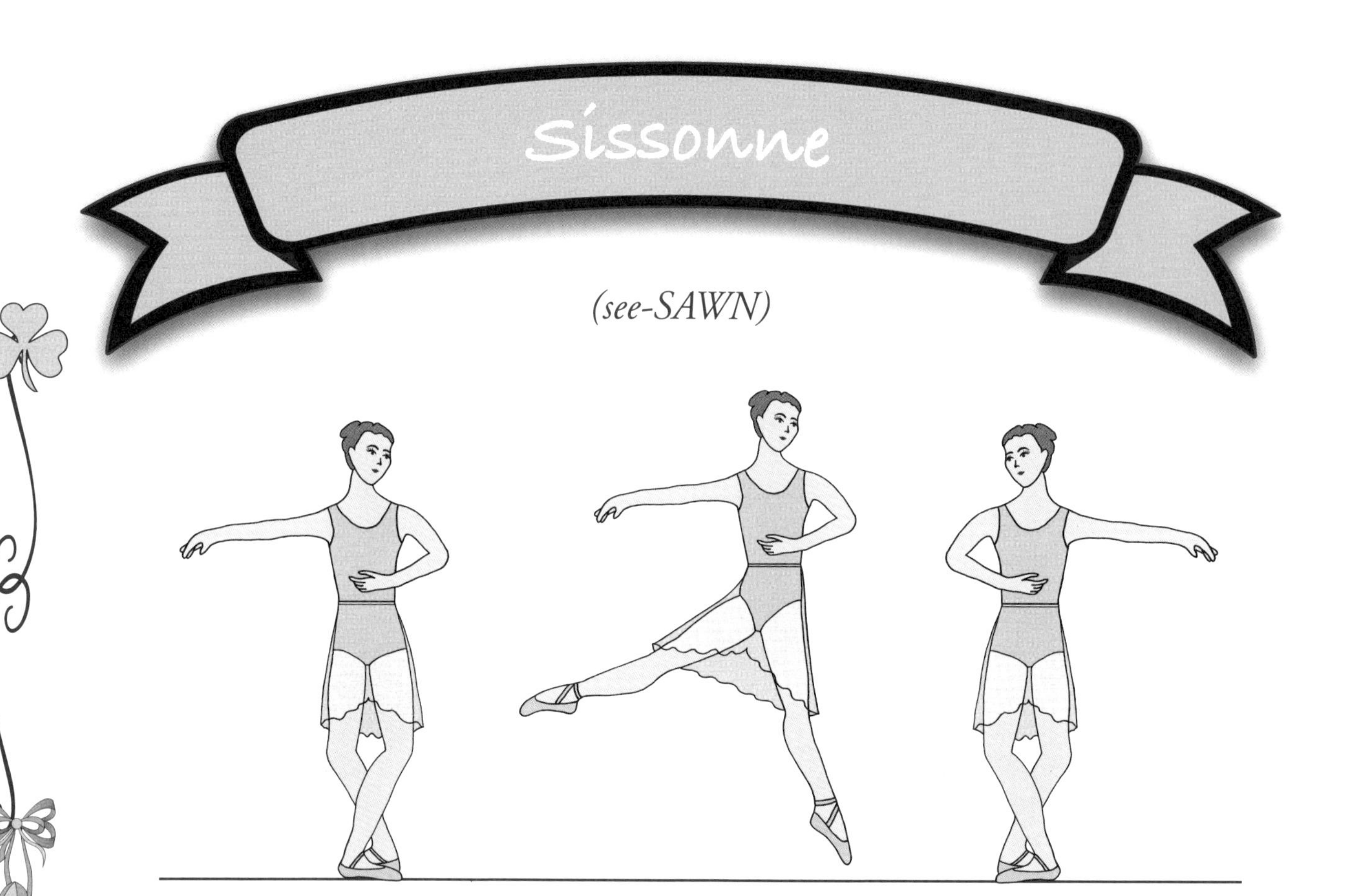

Sissonne - named for the originator of the step.

A jump from two feet to one foot. Spring off of two feet propelling your body to the side. When traveling to the left, land on your left foot and then the right foot will close fifth. Sissonne may be executed:

de coté - **side (pictured)**

en avant - **forward or**

en arriere - **backward**

The second foot may close (fermé) or remain open (ouverte).

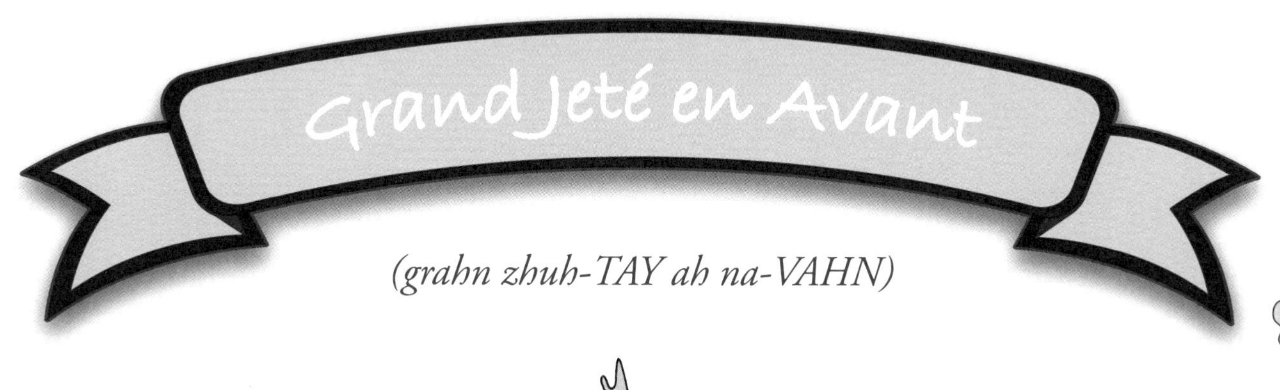

(grahn zhuh-TAY ah na-VAHN)

Large jeté forward.
Grand jeté is a large leap that begins by the front leg being thrown forward as in grand battement. The second leg extends back as in a grand battement to the back. The leap is high into the air and suspended for a moment before coming down.

Pirouette en Dehors

(peer-WET ahn duh-AWR)

Spin outside.

Prepare for the pirouette with the legs in a small fourth position plié. Relevé and turn on the front foot with the back foot quickly rising to retiré front.

A pirouette en dehors always turns away (outside) from the standing leg. When spinning on the right leg, the body will turn left. When spinning on the left leg, the body will turn right.

This describes the most common beginning *en dehors pirouette.* A pirouette may prepare in any position and spin in any position such as arabesque, attitude, or à la seconde.

Pirouette en Dedans

(peer-WET ahn duh-DAHN)

Spin inside.
Prepare for the pirouette in a fourth position lunge. (The front leg in plié and the back leg straight.) Relevé on the front foot and turn with the back leg rising to retiré front.
A pirouette en dedans always turns toward the standing leg (inside). When spinning on the right leg, the body will turn right. When spinning on the left leg, the body will turn left.

This describes the most common beginning *en dedans pirouette.* A pirouette may prepare in any position and spin in any position such as arabesque, attitude, or à la seconde.

Soutenu en tournant

(soot-NEW-ahn toor NAHN)

Sustained in turning.
The soutenu is the action of pulling in from fondu up to sous-sus. The turning comes by pivoting on your toes toward your back foot. This turning in sous-sus is called détourné. A soutenu en tournant is a soutenu plus a détourné. The action of the turn results in the opposite foot ending in the front in sous-sus.

Piqué Tour

(pee-KAY toor)

Pricked turn.

In a piqué turn, step on to a fully stretched leg to pointe or demi-pointe. The other leg is usually in retiré derriere, but may be in many different positions such as attitude or arabesque. Turn toward the standing leg one or multiple times, and close fifth to finish.

Chaînés Tours

(Shey NAYs toor)

Chains (links) turns.
Chaînés are done in first position on pointes or demi-pointes. Each turn consists of two steps, each step is a 1/2 rotation. Each step is equal in length and equal in timing.

Cabriole

(ka-bree-AWL)

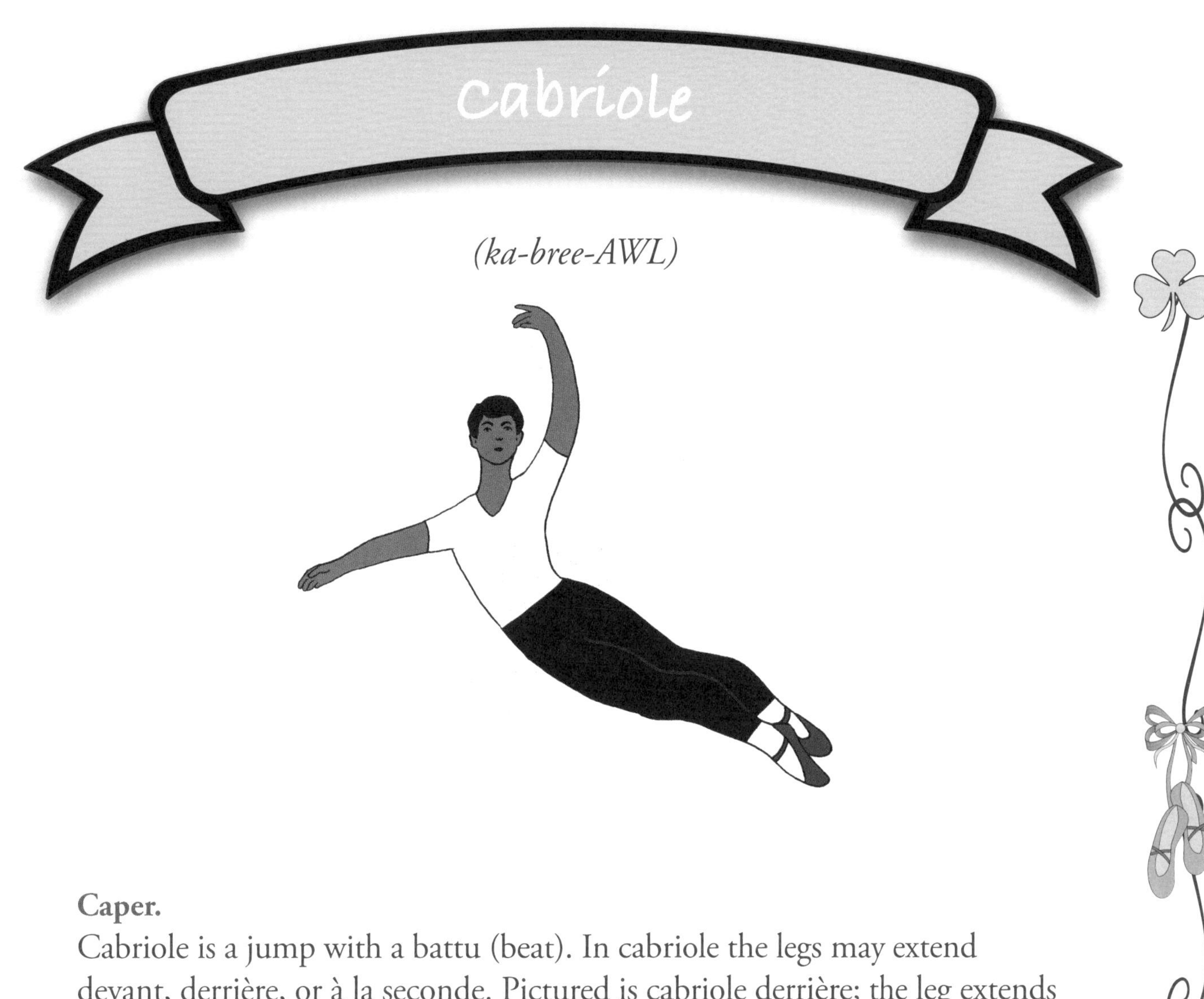

Caper.

Cabriole is a jump with a battu (beat). In cabriole the legs may extend devant, derrière, or à la seconde. Pictured is cabriole derrière; the leg extends to the back in arabesque (with fondu). Next the standing leg comes up to the top leg and beats from underneath. To finish the second leg returns to the floor to land in the original arabesque. Cabriole can be a small delicate step by women, or a very large jump with high elevation by men.

Pirouette à la seconde

(peer-WET ah la suh-GAWND)

Spin in second.

This is an advanced pirouette often performed by men with multiple rotations. The pirouette may prepare in second or fourth positions. The leg is fully extended to the second for the entire rotation of the turn while the standing leg is in relevé. To finish the standing heel is lowered while the leg is still extended, and then the working leg may close into a finishing pose.

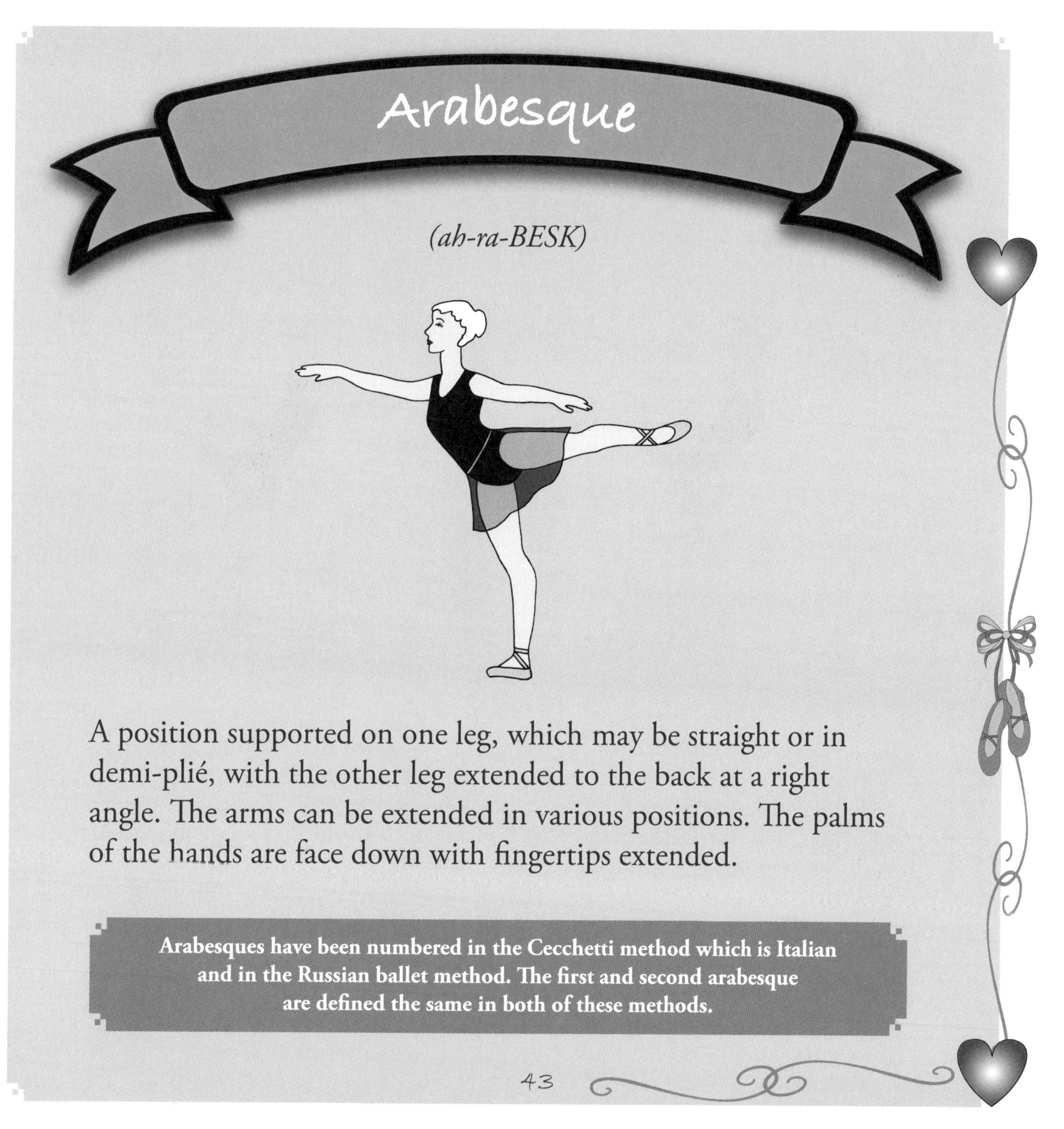

Arabesque

(ah-ra-BESK)

A position supported on one leg, which may be straight or in demi-plié, with the other leg extended to the back at a right angle. The arms can be extended in various positions. The palms of the hands are face down with fingertips extended.

Arabesques have been numbered in the Cecchetti method which is Italian and in the Russian ballet method. The first and second arabesque are defined the same in both of these methods.

Arabesque

(ah-ra-BESK)

First Arabesque

The legs are in an open position. The arm of the supporting leg is forward, the other arm and leg are back. The shoulders are held square with the line of the arms. The head is forward.

Second Arabesque

The legs are in an open position like first arabesque. The arms are reversed so that the arm of the working leg is forward. The head is slightly tilted toward the audience.

To understand an open position, refer to effacé on page 50.

Arabesque

(ah-ra-BESK)

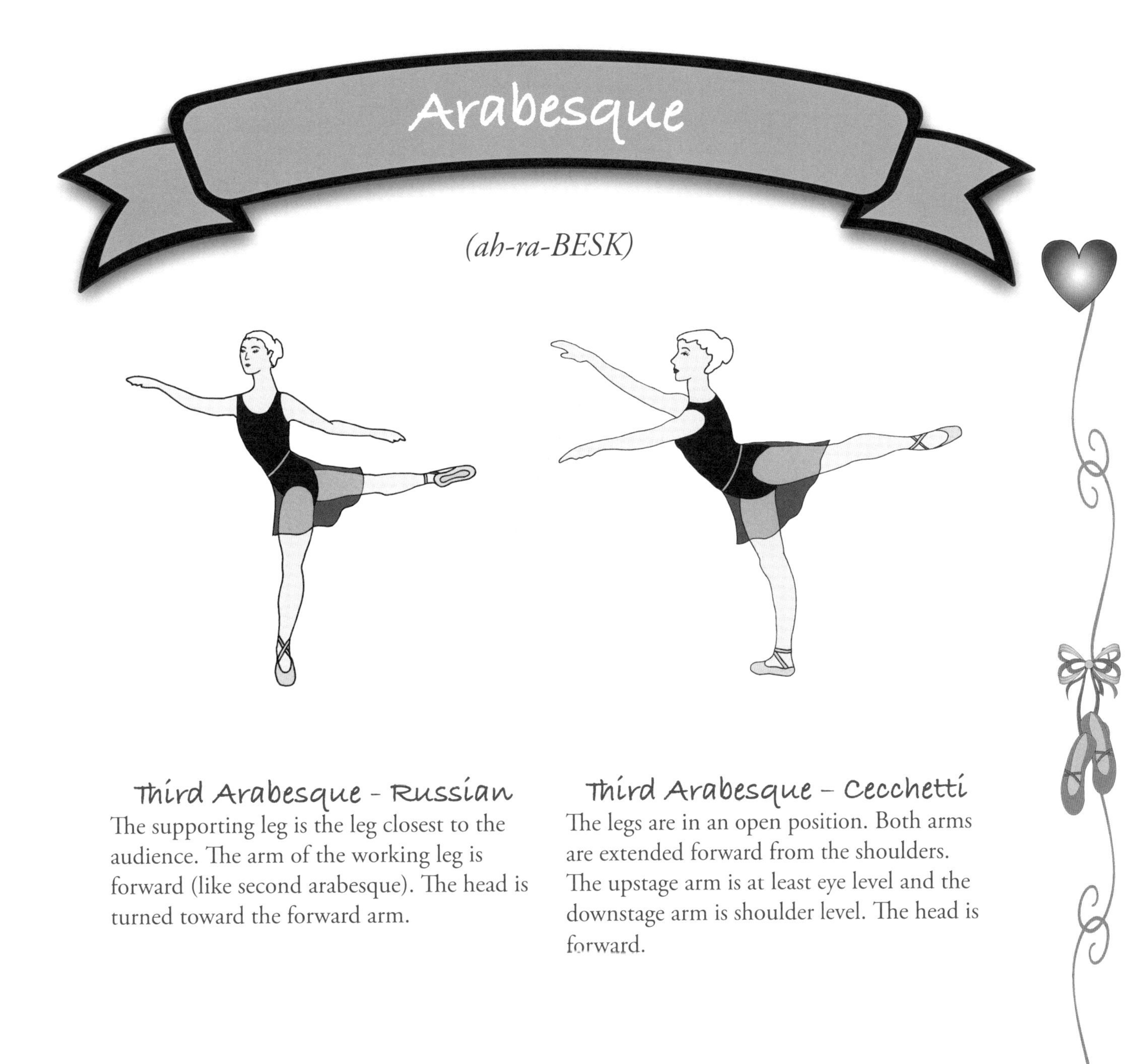

Third Arabesque - Russian

The supporting leg is the leg closest to the audience. The arm of the working leg is forward (like second arabesque). The head is turned toward the forward arm.

Third Arabesque - Cecchetti

The legs are in an open position. Both arms are extended forward from the shoulders. The upstage arm is at least eye level and the downstage arm is shoulder level. The head is forward.

Arabesque

(ah-ra-BESK)

Fourth Arabesque – Russian

The supporting leg is the leg closest to the audience. The arm of the supporting leg is forward. The back is shown to the audience by a strong arching of the back. The head is turned toward the audience.

Body Facings

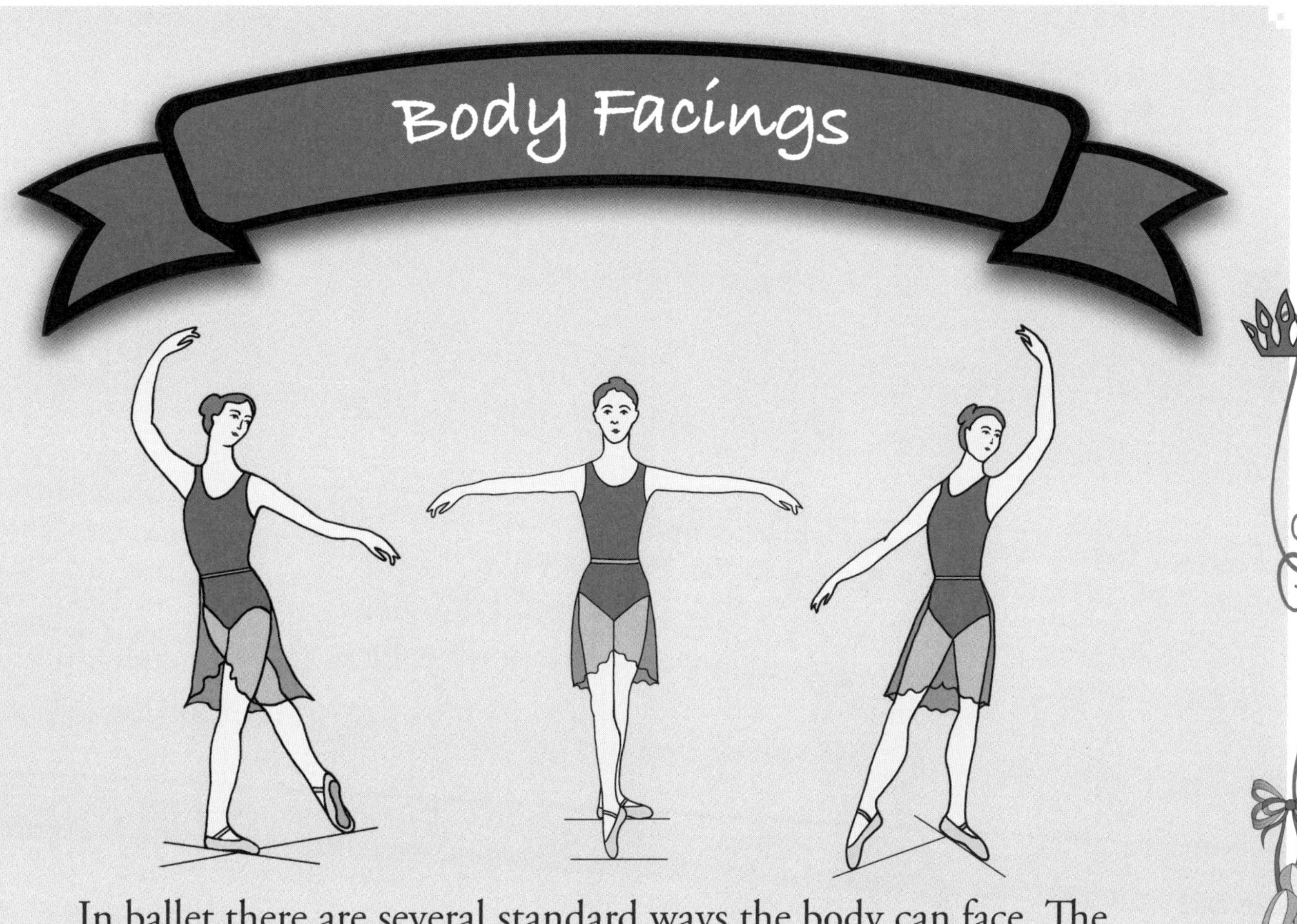

In ballet there are several standard ways the body can face. The body will either be facing one of the 4 walls or one of the 4 corners. The body facing tells the dancer which wall or corner to face, which direction the leg goes, and where the arms and head are placed. The illustrations in this section picture the body facing in tendu, but the leg could be in other positions. These directional terms apply to any position or action.

Croisé Devant

(krwah-ZAY duh-VAHN)

Crossed in front.

The body is facing one of the front corners and the downstage leg is to the front. (See how the legs are crossed.) The arms are in third opposition. The front leg may execute any movement like tendu, développé, or attitude.

Opposition is a term in dance that means you use the opposite arm from the leg. If the right leg is front, then the left arm will be front or up.

(ah la ka-tree-EM duh-VAHN)

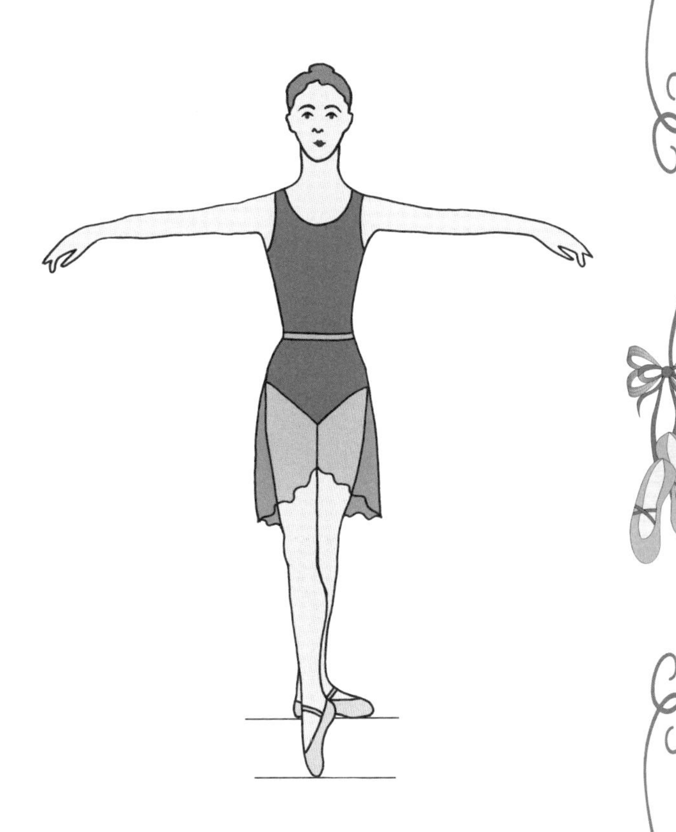

To the fourth in front.

The body is facing the audience. The working leg is in a position to the fourth in front like tendu or battement.

En Face (ahn fahss)
Facing or opposite.
En face is a term that means the body is directly facing or opposite the audience. À la quatrième devant is an en face position.

Effacé Devant

(eh-fa-SAY duh-VAHN)

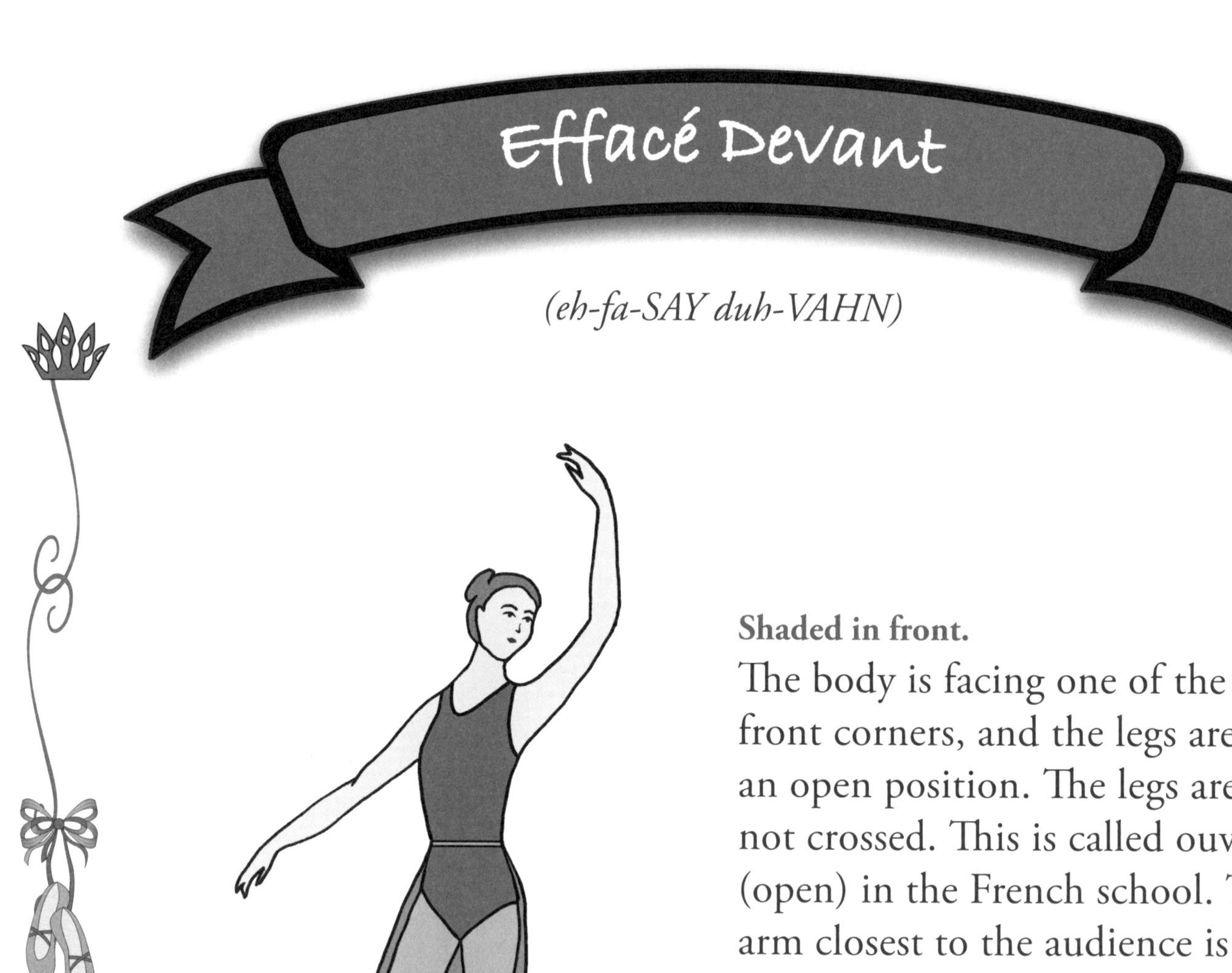

Shaded in front.

The body is facing one of the front corners, and the legs are in an open position. The legs are not crossed. This is called ouverte (open) in the French school. The arm closest to the audience is high, "shading" the face.

Écarté Devant

(ay-kar-TAY duh-VAHN)

Thrown wide apart front.

Écarté is a position where the dancer is in second (to the side) along the diagonal line. In devant the working leg is pointed on the front diagonal. The arm on the side of the working leg is in fifth. The head looks toward the front hand.

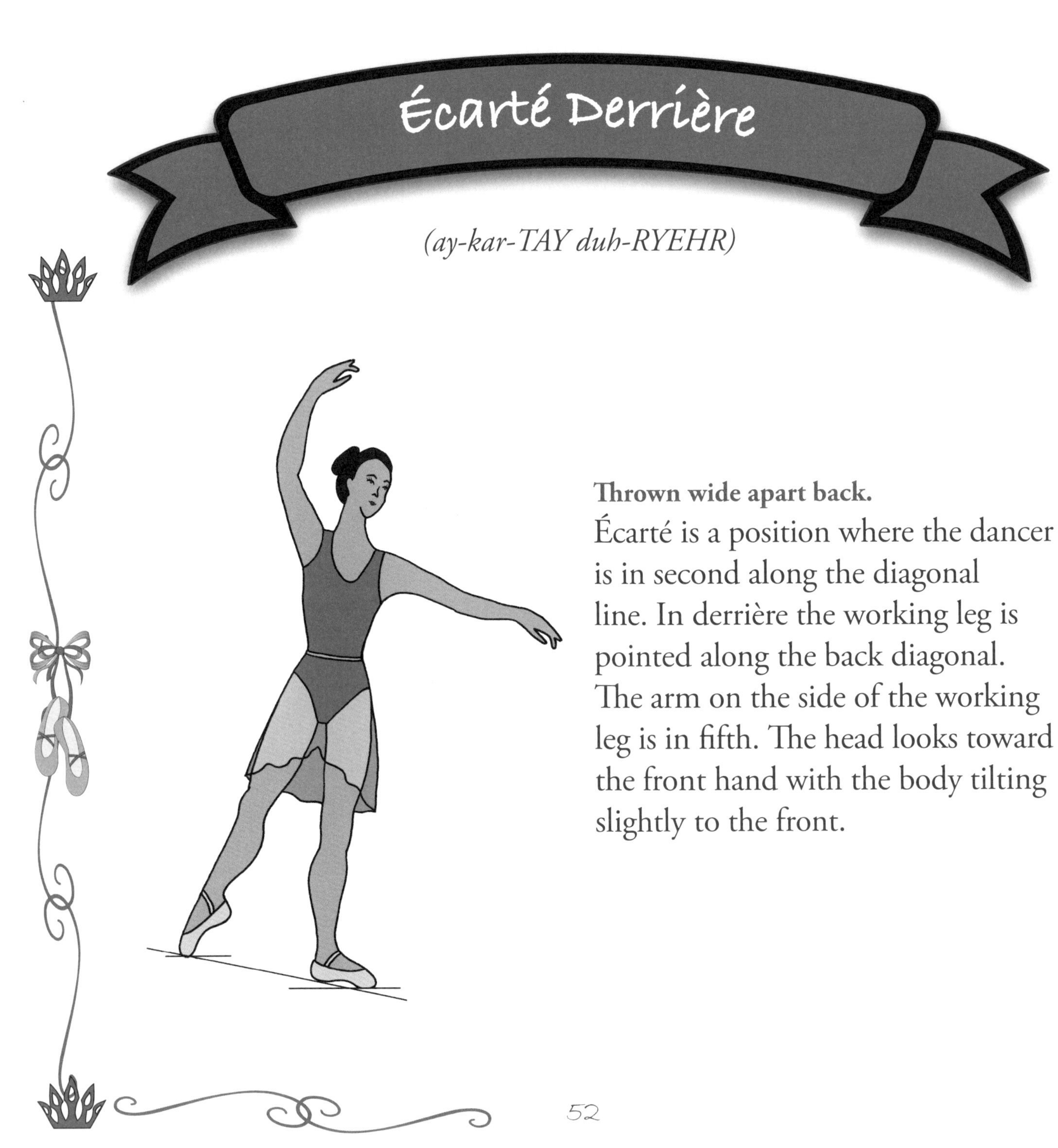

Écarté Derrière

(ay-kar-TAY duh-RYEHR)

Thrown wide apart back.

Écarté is a position where the dancer is in second along the diagonal line. In derrière the working leg is pointed along the back diagonal. The arm on the side of the working leg is in fifth. The head looks toward the front hand with the body tilting slightly to the front.

À la Seconde

(ah la suh-GAWND)

To the Second.

The foot is extended to the second (side). This position is en face (facing the audience). The arms are in second position. The head is straight forward.

(eh-fa-SAY duh-RYEHR)

Shaded back.

In this body facing, the dancer faces one of the front corners. The downstage leg is extended to the fourth in back. The legs are not crossed. This is called ouverte (open) in the French school. The arm closest to the audience is in fifth, "shading" the dancer from the audience.

À la Quatrième Derrière

(ah la ka-tree-EM duh-RYEHR)

To the fourth in back.

The body is facing the audience. (en face) The working leg is placed to the fourth in back. The arms are in seconde. The head is straight forward.

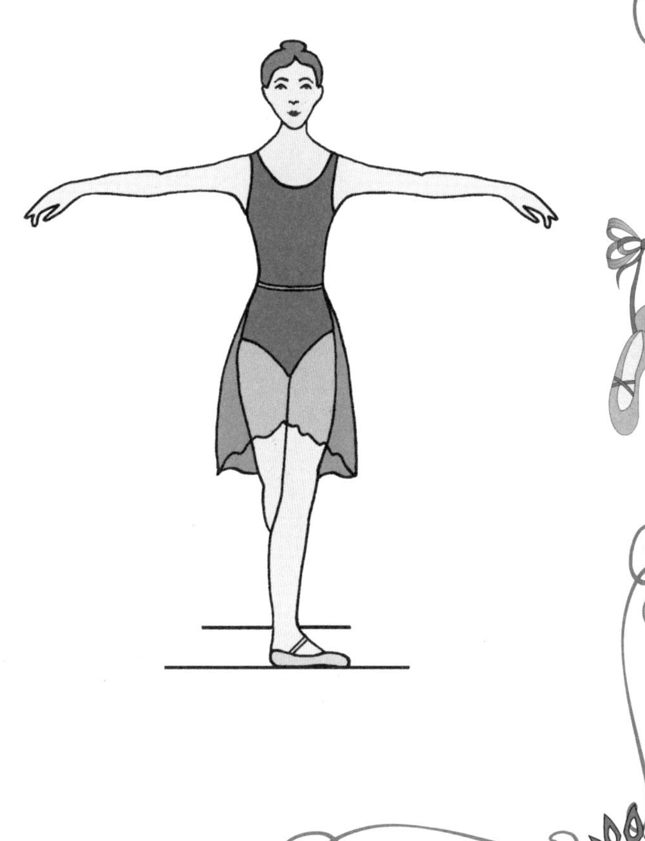

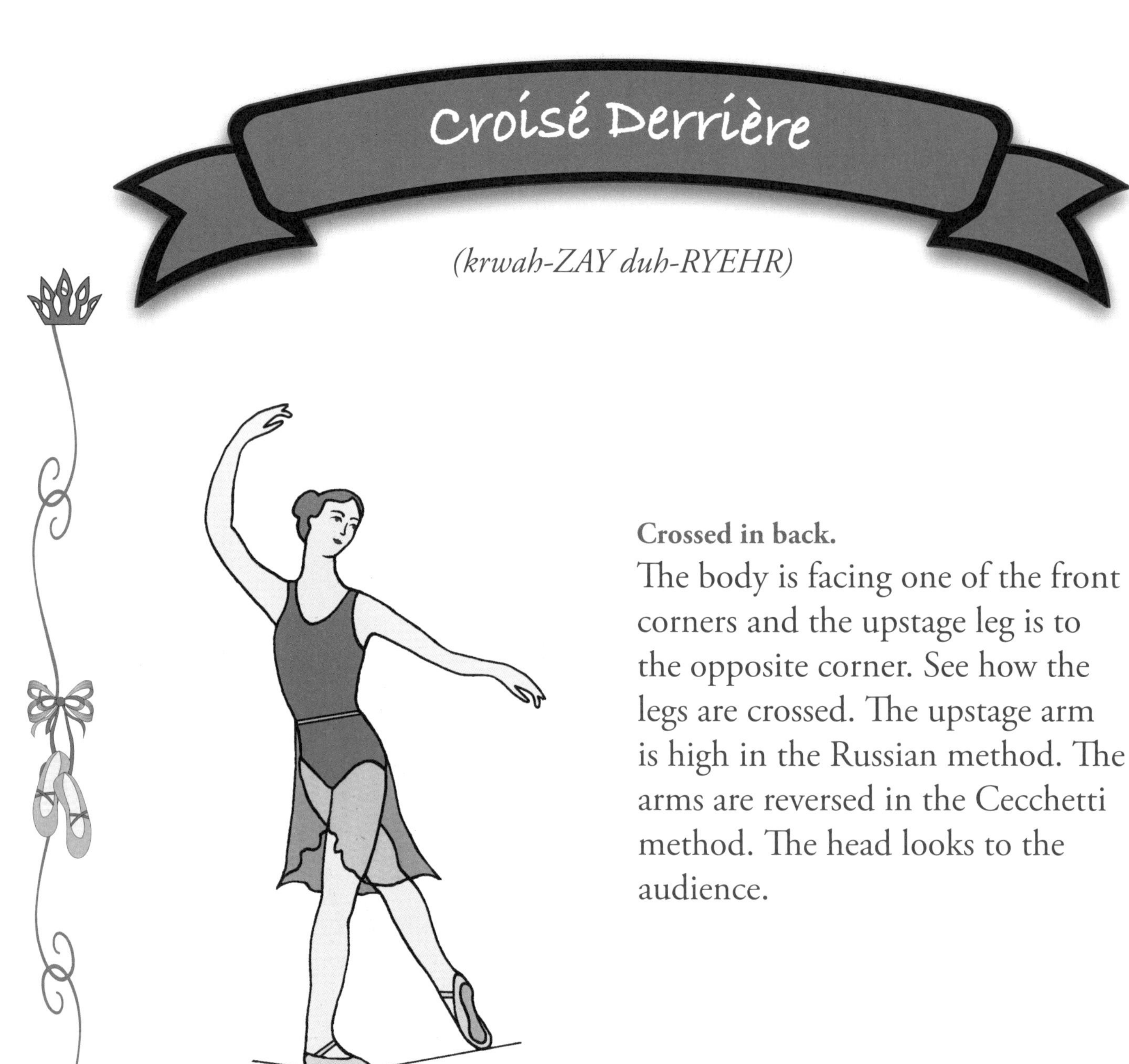

Croisé Derrière

(krwah-ZAY duh-RYEHR)

Crossed in back.

The body is facing one of the front corners and the upstage leg is to the opposite corner. See how the legs are crossed. The upstage arm is high in the Russian method. The arms are reversed in the Cecchetti method. The head looks to the audience.

Révérence

(ray-vay-RAHNSS)

Révérence is a formal bow to end the ballet class. The students bow to the teacher and to the accompanist if there is one. This is a beautiful way to show appreciation. The révérence may be a simple curtsy for females and bow for males when students are young, or a longer combination and deep bow when they are older.

Index

Index